FORCES AND MOTION

Simon de Pinna

Photography by
Chris Fairclough

WAYLAND

Produced for Wayland Publishers Ltd by
The Creative Publishing Company Ltd
Unit 3, 37 Watling Street, Leintwardine
Shropshire SY7 0LW, England

First published in 1997 by
Wayland Publishers Ltd,
61 Western Road, Hove,
East Sussex BN3 1JD, England

British Library Cataloguing in Publication Data
Pinna, Simon de. 1954-
  Forces and Motion. - (Science Projects)
  1. Force and energy - Juvenile literature
  2. Motion - Juvenile literature
  1. Title
  531.6

ISBN 0 7502 2050 3

Printed and bound in Italy by
G. Canale & C.S.p.A., Turin

Designer: Ian Winton
Editors: Patience Coster and Paul Humphrey
Consultant: Jeremy Bloomfield
Illustrations: Mick Gillah
Cover and p19 Julian Baker

Picture acknowledgements
The publishers would like to thank the following
for permission to reproduce their pictures
Bruce Coleman: pages 33 (Peter Terry), 36 (Erwin
and Peggy Bauer); **Ford UK:** page 22; **NASA:** page
40; **Science Photo Library:** cover (James
Stevenson) and page 6; **Tony Stone Images**:
pages 4 (Ken Biggs), 9 (George Lepp), 10 (Richard
Kaylin), 12 (David Young Wolff), 14 (Lori Adamski
Peek), 16 (Nicholas Pinturas), 24 (Janet Gill), 26
(Andrea Booher), 30, 34 (Amwell), 38, 42 (Roger
Labrosse), 44 (Peter Newton).

The publishers would like to thank the staff and
pupils of Harborne Junior School, Birmingham, for
their help in the preparation of this book.

NATIONAL CURRICULUM NOTES

The investigations in this book are cross-referenced to Programmes of Study for Science at
Key Stages 2, 3 and 4.

FORCES EVERYWHERE Although forces cannot be seen,
everyone can recognize their effects (they make things move
or change their shape).

GRAVITY Objects have weight because of the gravitational
pull of the Earth; the gravitational attraction between two
objects depends on their masses. KS2 Sc4 2b

MAGNETIC FORCE There are forces of attraction and
repulsion between magnets; properties of magnetic materials.
KS2 Sc4 2a; KS4 Sc4 1r (double)

ELECTROSTATIC FORCE There are forces of attraction and
repulsion between unlike and like charges. KS3 Sc4 1b; KS4
Sc4 1n (double)

MEASURING FORCES The newton as a unit of force; the
extension of a spring is related to the force acting on it. KS2
Sc4 2d, and e; KS4 Sc4 2d (single)

RESISTANCE Inertia resisting movement or a change in
movement; friction as a force tending to decrease movement.
KS2 Sc4 2c; KS3 Sc4 2e

SLIPPERY SHAPES Drag as a frictional force in fluids; how
streamlined design reduces drag.

FLIGHT How the forces of thrust and lift resist the forces of
drag and gravity; aerodynamic design. KS2 Sc4 2f

SURFACE TENSION The force tending to keep the surface
area of a liquid to a minimum. KS3 Sc3 1b; KS4 Sc3 1m
(double)

UNDER PRESSURE The force exerted over a particular area
(solids and gases). KS2 Sc4 2f; KS3 Sc4 2h, and i

WATER PRESSURE The law of hydraulics and its
applications to braking systems etc. KS3 Sc4 2h, and i; KS4
Sc4 2k (double)

FLOATING AND SINKING Displacement and upthrust. KS2
Sc4 2g

MAKING TASKS EASIER The features of simple machines,
particularly levers. KS2 Sc4 2f; KS3 Sc4 2f, and g

BALANCING ACT Balancing forces; centres of gravity and
stability. KS2 Sc4 2f, and g; KS3 Sc4 2d, and f

STRONG SHAPES Cylinders, triangles and bridge design.
KS2 Sc4 2f, and g

ON THE MOVE An introduction to Newton's first and
second laws of motion. KS2 Sc4 2f, and h; KS3 Sc4 2c

SPEED The relation between speed, distance travelled and
time taken. How speed is measured. KS3 Sc4 2a, and b

FASTER AND SLOWER Acceleration. How acceleration is
measured. KS3 Sc4 2c; KS4 Sc4 2d (double)

ACTION AND REACTION Newton's third law of motion.
KS4 Sc4 2g (double)

COLLISIONS Momentum and its conservation. The
implications for car design. KS2 Sc4 2h; KS3 Sc4 2c; KS4 Sc4
2g

ROUND AND ROUND Circular motion and centripetal force.

CONTENTS

FORCES EVERYWHERE

What are forces? Forces can launch rockets into space and split the Earth apart in an earthquake. They can slow objects down, speed them up or change the direction in which they are moving. They can even change the shape of an object. If there were no forces, nothing would ever happen. But sometimes forces seem to be doing nothing at all: this could be because the effect of one force is balanced by the effect of another, like two people at either end of a see-saw.

Forces cannot be seen, but you experience their effects all the time. Your weight is a force: for example, when you get out of bed in the morning, your weight pulls you towards the floor. Sit at the top of a slide and the force of gravity will pull you down. You don't move far beyond the end of the slide because the force of friction slows you down when you hit the ground!

There are pulling, pushing and turning forces in action all around us.

There are many words used to describe the different forces in action around us. We use words such as magnetic force, electrostatic force, gravitational force, squashing, stretching and bending. However, this range of words serves to describe just three different forces: pushing, pulling and turning.

Did you know?

The great forces at work during earthquakes are recorded using two scales. The 12-point Mercalli scale is based on what is seen and felt during an earthquake, and ranges from 'can be recorded but not felt' to 'total destruction'. The Richter scale is a 10-point scale that measures the energy in a tremor. The strongest earthquake ever occurred in Tokyo, Japan in 1923, and measured just under 9 on the Richter scale.

STORY TIME

MATERIALS
- a pencil
- a notebook

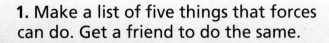

1. Make a list of five things that forces can do. Get a friend to do the same.

2. Swap lists. The first person to make up a story that mentions all the forces on their list is the winner!

FORCE WORDS

MATERIALS
- a pencil
- a notebook

1. Sit in a circle with your friends.

2. Take it in turns to say an 'action' word that has something to do with forces or movement, such as bend, twist, run, climb, lift, squeeze. You could try acting out the words, too.

3. Whoever cannot think of a word within a count of ten must drop out. The last person left in is the winner.

GRAVITY

The Moon has enough gravity to hold astronauts on to its surface, but they have far less weight there than on Earth.

how far from the Earth the force reached. Newton realized that the force might extend to the Moon, which would explain why the Moon stayed in orbit around the Earth.

The Earth's gravity pulls you downwards with a certain amount of force. You call this amount your weight. The Moon has far less mass than the Earth, so its gravity is much weaker. Astronauts on the Moon have only one sixth of their weight on Earth, although their mass does not change.

There is a well known saying: 'What goes up must come down'. Why is this so? The answer is gravity. Gravity is a force that pulls all objects towards each other. The size of the force depends on the mass of the object doing the pulling. Mass is a word scientists use to describe the amount of matter (or stuff) that makes up an object. The Earth has far more mass than an apple, so the gravitational pull of the Earth is much greater than the pull of the apple!

The famous scientist Sir Isaac Newton came to this conclusion more than three hundred years ago, when he saw an apple fall from a tree in his garden. This set him thinking about the force that made it happen and he wondered

Newton went on to show that the gravitational force between the planets and the Sun is great enough to hold them together in our solar system, even while they are moving through space. We now know that gravity keeps everything in the Universe in place, from moons and planets to stars and galaxies.

Did you know?

Astronomers say there is a type of star that shrinks under the influence of its own gravitational force. Eventually, it becomes so small that even light made by the star itself cannot escape the pull of its gravity. The star has become a 'black hole', able to suck matter into itself from nearby stars.

WEIGHT WATCHERS

1. Hold a ball-bearing and a marble of similar size in each hand. Which one feels heavier?

2. Roll out some modelling clay on the board to make a slab about 5 mm thick. Place the board on the floor.

3. Stand over the clay and drop the two balls at the same time from the same height. Does one ball hit the clay first or do they both hit it together? What does the answer to this question tell you about how the weight of the balls affects the speed at which they fall?

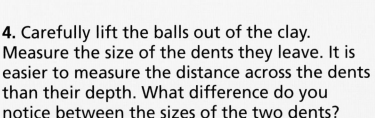

4. Carefully lift the balls out of the clay. Measure the size of the dents they leave. It is easier to measure the distance across the dents than their depth. What difference do you notice between the sizes of the two dents?

5. Try the experiment again with ball-bearings or marbles of different sizes. Does the size of an object affect how fast it falls?

7

MAGNETIC FORCE

Magnets are pieces of material, usually with iron in them, that attract or repel other pieces of iron with what we call a magnetic force, or magnetism. The Ancient Chinese knew that lumps of a certain type of black, magnetic rock, called lodestone, could attract or repel each other, depending on the direction in which they were turned, and would point north if allowed to swing freely. The Ancient Chinese were the first people to use lodestones as compasses to guide ships to their destinations.

If you hang a bar magnet from a thread, it will act in the same way as a lodestone, with one end pointing towards the North pole and the other towards the South. This is why one end of a magnet is called the north (or north-seeking) pole and the other end is called the south (or south-seeking) pole. When two magnets are brought together, the north pole of one will attract the south pole of the other, but it will repel a similar north pole. This rule about magnets is often summed up as: 'Unlike poles attract and like poles repel'. The area around a magnet where these effects happen is called the magnetic field.

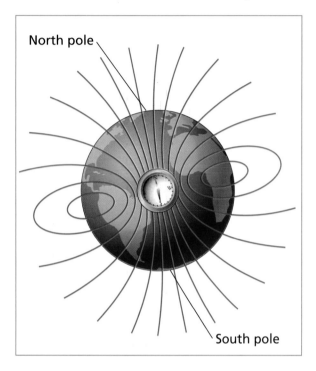

North pole

South pole

The Earth is a giant magnet. It attracts other magnets, such as compass needles, so that they line up with the poles. The red lines show the Earth's magnetic field.

HUNT THE MAGNET

1. Hide one of the bar magnets inside the shoebox.

2. Get a friend to move the compass over the lid of the box and watch the needle turn to point towards the north pole of the magnet.

3. Can your friend work out the position of the hidden magnet?

MATERIALS
- a compass
- 2 bar magnets
- an empty shoebox
- a pencil

Did you know?

The spectacular aurora borealis, or northern lights, is an ever-changing pattern of white or multi-coloured lights. It is caused by particles in the atmosphere which are attracted towards the Earth's magnetic poles. In the southern hemisphere there is a similar display, called the aurora australis.

4. Mark the spot they choose with a cross and see how close to the magnet they get.

5. Now ask your friend to hide two magnets, and you try hunting them. This can be much harder!

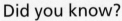

ELECTROSTATIC FORCE

When you comb your hair, you often see individual hairs stand on end and move towards the comb: there seems to be a force attracting the hairs towards it. This is called electrostatic force and it is an example of what static electricity can do. Electrostatic force makes dust cling to a television screen and drags ink powder on to the paper in a photocopier. When you take off a nylon sweater in the dark, the sparks you see are caused by static electricity.

Electrostatic force is produced when you rub two materials, such as a plastic balloon and a nylon sweater, together. The force occurs between materials that carry what is called an

The flashes of lightning you see during a thunderstorm are huge sparks caused by static electricity.

electric charge. The act of rubbing knocks electrons – subatomic particles that carry a negative charge – off the sweater, and they stick to the atoms of the balloon. The atoms of the sweater are left with a positive charge. As with the poles of magnets, there is a law of physics that says 'opposite charges attract'; therefore, the negatively-charged balloon sticks to the positively-charged sweater. The law also says that 'like charges repel': so, if two negatively-charged balloons are brought close together, the electrostatic force pushes them apart.

SILVER DANCERS

1. Rub the disc several times with the cloth, using a circular motion. This puts a negative charge on the disc.

2. Carefully place the disc over the bowl and put twelve silver balls on the surface. They will roll about for a few seconds and then stop.

3. Move the point of the pencil towards one of the balls. What happens to the ball?

MATERIALS

- an old (not precious!) vinyl LP disc
- a plastic or glass bowl
- silver balls used for decorating cakes
- a sharp pencil
- a dry cloth

WATER MAGIC

1. Rub the plastic ruler against the sweater. After rubbing several times, the ruler will carry a negative charge.

2. Hold the ruler near a gentle stream of water. What happens, and why? Don't let the ruler get wet, or the effect will disappear.

3. Try the experiment again using the other materials in turn. Note the effect that each one has on the stream of water.

MATERIALS

- a plastic ruler
- a copper rod
- a pencil
- a wooden ruler or dowel rod
- a steel ruler
- a sweater
- a tap

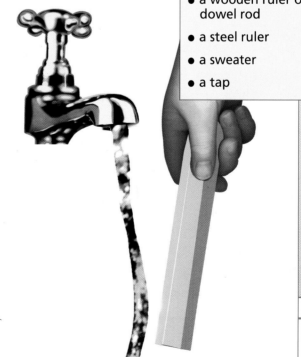

MEASURING FORCES

Forces are measured in units called newtons, named after Isaac Newton. If you hold a 1 kilogram (1 kg) bag of sugar in your hand, gravity is pulling down on the bag with a force of very nearly 10 newtons, or 10 N for short. So, if your mass is 50 kg, the Earth is pulling on you with a force of 500 N, which is how scientists describe your weight. Confusingly, when you weigh things in shops, the weighing scales are usually marked in kilograms – the units of mass. It is easy to make the mistake of calling that measurement 'weight'.

Instruments used to measure forces are called forcemeters; if they are marked in newtons, they are called newtonmeters. The weighing scales in the supermarket or your bathroom scales are fairly inaccurate forcemeters, but most of them work in the same way as scientific newtonmeters, that is by either stretching or squashing a spring.

Supermarket weighing scales measure mass, not weight. The more mass an object has, the more strongly it is pulled towards the Earth by gravity.

MAKE A FORCEMETER

1. Cut out a strip of card and stick it or tack it along one edge of the wooden board.

2. Hammer the nail into the board, towards one end. Loop an elastic band around the nail and stand the board upright. With the pencil, draw a line on the card opposite the lowest point of the elastic band.

MATERIALS

- a wooden board 30 cm x 15 cm
- elastic bands and springs of various sizes
- a ruler and a pencil
- stiff card
- a small nail
- a hammer
- weighing scales marked in grams and kilograms
- a plastic bag
- flour or rice
- thread
- scissors
- glue or thumb tacks

3. Weigh out 100 g of flour or rice into the plastic bag and tie a length of thread around the neck of the bag to seal it.

4. Tie the thread on to the bottom of the elastic band and, with the board upright, mark the card opposite the new lowest point of the elastic band. Next to this point on the card, write '1 N'. (Remember: a mass of 1 kg has a weight of 10 N on Earth.)

> **WARNING!**
> - Take care when using the hammer and nail.

5. Repeat steps **3** and **4** with bags weighing 200 g, 300 g and so on, to make a force scale that can measure up to 10 N. The elastic band force measurer is only accurate when the distances between each mark on the scale are the same. By looking at the marks on your scale, you should be able to tell the smallest and largest forces your elastic band can measure.

6. Find five objects that you think your force measurer can weigh. Arrange them in order of weight by holding them in your hands. Now record the weights of the objects by hanging them from the thread on the elastic band. Was the order you guessed correct?

7. Experiment with other elastic bands and springs as force measurers. Which are more accurate at weighing, springs or elastic bands?

RESISTANCE

Have you seen the trick in which a conjuror quickly pulls a cloth from beneath a number of items on a table without breaking anything? Everything stays on the table in more or less the same position it was in before the trick. The reason for this is that all objects will resist a force trying to move them. This 'unwillingness' to move is called inertia. The force needed to overcome the inertia of an object depends on the mass of the object. The objects laid on the table have sufficient inertia to resist the force of the moving tablecloth.

Inertia also keeps objects moving. Once launched into space, a spacecraft will travel forever until a force acts upon it. For the same reason, a moving object will resist any force that might alter the speed at which it is going or change its direction. Newton discovered this, and it became the first of his three laws of motion.

Resistance to movement comes not only from the inertia of the object itself, but also from whatever surface it is moving over. A ball rolling across a football pitch will soon slow down and stop because of the resistance of the grass to the ball. The rougher the surface, the greater this force of resistance, or friction.

Skiers often use wax to reduce the friction between the snow and their skis; it helps them travel faster.

When objects need to move quickly, friction can be a nuisance. For example, the moving parts of a car engine change a lot of the energy into wasteful heat when they rub against each other. Oil is added to the engine to reduce the friction between its moving parts. But friction can save lives. The force between the tread of a car's tyres and the road slows down and stops it. In wet or icy conditions, the friction force is reduced and tyres lose their grip.

SLIP AND GRIP

1. Draw a line across the board about 30 cm from one end and hammer the nails into the board, one at each end of the line. The nails will stop the test materials slipping down the ramp.

2. Place a shoe on the board, making the toe of the shoe level with the line. Raise this end of the board until the shoe just starts to slide. At this point, the force of gravity is slightly greater than the friction force between the ramp and the shoe (the inertia of the shoe is small enough to ignore). Keeping the ramp at this angle, make a note of the height of the end of the board.

3. Repeat the test, placing the shoe on each of the different friction test materials in turn. Draw a bar chart on the squared paper to show the different ramp heights. What effect do the different materials have on the size of the friction force?

4. How does the material used to make the soles of the shoes, or the pattern on the soles, affect the friction force? Use the range of shoes you have collected to investigate these questions.

SLIPPERY SHAPES

By testing models in a wind tunnel, designers can find the best shapes to reduce drag.

Motorbikes and cars, especially those used for racing, have shiny, rounded surfaces. This design makes the air flow smoothly over the vehicle and reduces drag. Motorbike riders also have to make themselves as streamlined as possible by wearing skin-tight clothing and rounded crash helmets.

Water produces more drag than air. Designing a ship's hull is a complicated task, because the streamlined shapes that would increase its speed might also make it unstable. Ships need fins to make them stable, but these tend to increase drag. In ship-building the calculations are so precise that designers often use computers to help them find the best shape.

The force of friction not only resists movement over solid surfaces, it also occurs when objects move through fluids – liquids and gases. This type of friction is called drag.

Drag is sometimes useful, and sometimes not. Parachutists depend on the drag between the air and their parachutes to land safely. But people who design machines to move through air or water are usually very keen to keep drag forces as small as possible. This is because the more slippery, or streamlined, a vehicle's shape, the faster or further it will travel on a given amount of fuel.

Did you know?

Even trucks need to be streamlined! Their cabs are fitted with plastic scoops and deflectors to reduce the amount of fuel they use. They do this by forcing the air to pass smoothly over the top or around the sides of the truck, so reducing drag.

SHIP SHAPE

1. Place the guttering on a level table or other surface where the end of the gutter overhangs a drop of at least 1 m. Place the bricks or books on either side of the gutter to support it.

2. File a small groove in the middle of the overhanging end-stop. Carefully pour water into the gutter until it is three-quarters full.

3. Cut 2.4 m of thread or line and tie one end to the bag of sand or rice. Attach the other end to the hook on one of the boat shapes.

4. Place the boat shape in the water and slide the line through the groove to the bag. Hold the boat at the far end of the gutter and let it go. Start the clock and record the time it takes the boat to reach the end of the gutter.

5. Repeat the test for all the shapes. You should do each one more than once and work out the average times. Which shape has the most drag? Which is most streamlined?

MATERIALS

- a 2-m length of rain guttering fitted with watertight end-stops
- a stopwatch
- a round file
- a small plastic bag containing rice or sand to act as a weight
- hull shapes cut out from a piece of pine and fitted with small screw-in eyelets or cup hooks
- 2 bricks or large books
- nylon thread or fishing line

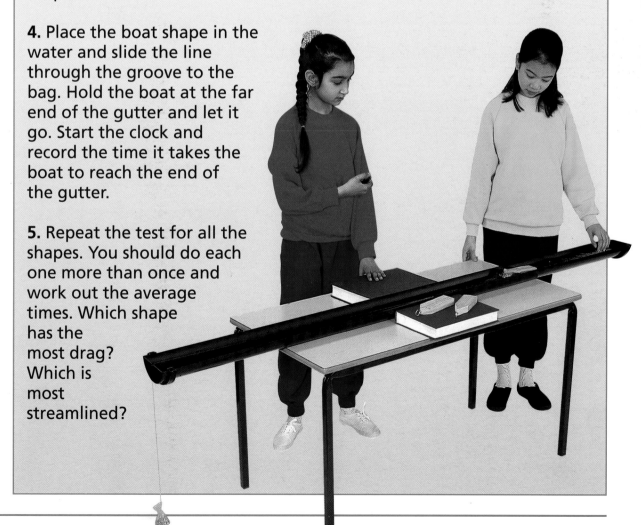

FLIGHT

To get any object off the ground and keep it moving through the air, there are four forces to consider. These are *weight* and *drag* which slow the object down, and *thrust* and *lift* which tend to speed it up.

Most modern aircraft fly using jet propulsion. The engines of a jet aircraft suck in air at the front. They squash, or compress, the air so that it gets very hot and they burn fuel in it. The burning mixture expands rapidly and rushes out of the rear of the engines, producing a huge thrust force.

Lift is a force produced when air moves over a surface, such as a wing or a propeller. The faster the aircraft flies, the greater the difference between the speed of the air flowing above and below the wing – and the greater the lift.

HIGH FLYERS

1. Cut out the wing, rudder and tailplane shapes from the card or balsa-wood. Cut two 20 cm lengths and two 3 cm lengths of balsa-wood and glue them together to make a frame for the fuselage of the plane.

2. Use a thin drill or bradawl to make a hole in each end of the wooden frame. Straighten the paper clips and thread the first through one end of the frame. Bend the end of the wire on the inside of the frame to make a hook.

MATERIALS

- a sheet of thin card or balsa-wood
- 50 cm of 1 cm square-section balsa-wood
- a model propeller
- a large elastic band
- modelmaker's glue
- 2 large paper clips
- a round bead
- a craft knife
- a drill or bradawl
- modelling clay

WARNING!

- Take care when using the craft knife.

3. On the outside of the frame, thread the bead and the propeller on to the wire and bend over the wire to secure them. Make sure the propeller can spin easily.

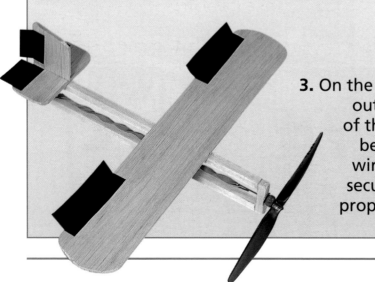

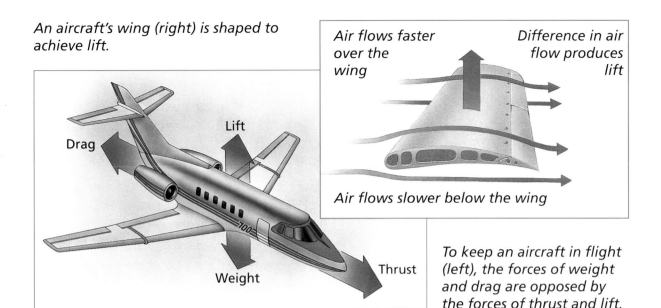

An aircraft's wing (right) is shaped to achieve lift.

Lift

Drag

Weight

Thrust

Air flows faster over the wing

Difference in air flow produces lift

Air flows slower below the wing

To keep an aircraft in flight (left), the forces of weight and drag are opposed by the forces of thrust and lift.

4. Thread the other paper clip through the hole in the opposite end of the frame and bend over the end of the wire inside the frame to make a hook. Bend over the other end of the wire so that it cannot easily be pulled through.

5. Attach the elastic band between the two hooks so that it is slightly taut. Glue the wings, rudder and tailplane on to the frame.

6. Rest the model on a finger placed under the point where the wings are attached. If the plane does not stay level, add a small piece of modelling clay to the nose or the tail to make it balance.

7. Wind up the propeller until the elastic band is tight and, holding the plane just behind the wings, gently launch it into the air. How well does it fly?

8. Cut out some rectangles of card about 6 x 2 cm and glue them along the rear edges of the wings, rudder or tailplane to make flaps. Check that your plane still balances, adding modelling clay if necessary. How is its flight affected when you bend the flaps?

SURFACE TENSION

Surface tension is a pulling force. Liquids, such as falling rain and water dripping from a tap are pulled into round drops by surface tension. The effect of the force is to try to pull the surface in towards the centre of the drop. It seems to give the surface of the liquid a stretchy 'skin', like a balloon. If you fill a glass with water very carefully right to the brim, you can actually put in slightly more than the glass can hold. This is because surface tension pulls on the ultra-microscopic water molecules, keeping them in place and forming a mound of water, called a meniscus.

Again, if you carefully lay a paper clip on the surface, you will be able to see the 'dent' that the clip makes on the water. It is only by weakening the links that hold the water molecules together that the surface tension can be broken; then the water will spread out, and the paper clip will sink. So, in order to wet a greasy object, such as a dinner plate, the water's skin must first be broken; soap and detergent achieve this by reducing the attraction between the water molecules.

However, soap does not destroy surface tension completely. A soap bubble is an amount of gas enclosed in an elastic soapy 'skin'.

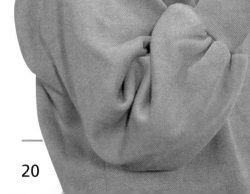

Surface tension is a force that pulls bubbles and drops of water into a round shape.

If you blow a bubble using a wire or plastic loop and stop blowing when the bubble is half-formed, it will shrink very rapidly and blow its air back at you! Surface tension is always trying to make bubbles smaller.

SURFACE TENSION BOAT

MATERIALS

- a sheet of card
- a pencil
- a ruler
- scissors
- glue
- a bar of soap
- a craft knife
- a washing-up bowl
- tracing paper
- water

1. First wash your hands! Any grease on them will stop the boat moving.

2. Trace the outline of the boat below on to the sheet of card.

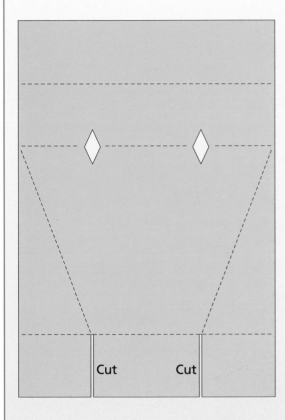

Cut   Cut

3. Cut along the solid lines and then fold the card along the dotted lines, starting with the sides.

4. Fold back the card at the front and rear of the boat. Glue the flaps where the front and sides overlap.

5. Cut out the two diamond shapes and wedge two small pieces of soap into the slits.

6. Half-fill a clean bowl with cold water and carefully place the boat on the surface. As the soap dissolves, it reduces the surface tension behind the boat and the greater surface tension force at the front pulls it forward. Watch your boat sail away!

UNDER PRESSURE

In science, pressure means how 'spread out' a force is. People make use of pressure in many situations. You can't push your thumb into a wooden board, for example, but you can push a drawing pin into it. You can do this because the force of your thumb pushing on the head of the pin is concentrated on a very small area under the point.

To work out the pressure under a force, you need to know two things: the size of the force, measured in newtons, and the area under the force. This can be written down as:

pressure = size of force ÷ by the area under the force

So, if a person weighing 600 newtons puts on a pair of skis that cover an area of 6,000 square centimetres, the pressure on the snow beneath the skier will be:

$600/6,000 = 0.1$ newtons per square centimetre, or 0.1 N per cm^2

When the skier takes off the skis, the area under her feet in normal shoes is only 600 square centimetres. This time the pressure will be:

$600/600 = 1$ N per cm^2

The pressure beneath the skier's feet is *ten times* greater now than it was when she had skis on. No wonder you sink into soft snow if you aren't wearing skis!

Everything that has weight exerts pressure. Water has pressure – the deeper you swim, the greater the water pressure. The air has pressure, too. In fact, the pressure of the atmosphere at ground level – about 10 N per cm^2 – would crush you, if it were not for the pressure of the gas and liquid inside your body, which balances the air pressure on the outside.

Pressurized air is used in this car airbag to keep the driver safe in a collision.

Changes in 'atmospheric pressure' (as the pressure of the air is called) are of great importance to pilots and weather forecasters. The higher you go, the lower the pressure. Aircraft altitude meters work by measuring the air pressure, while forecasters know that changes in air pressure can have dramatic effects on our weather. Many of us have devices called barometers in our homes; these predict changes in the weather by detecting small variations in atmospheric pressure and giving a reading on a dial.

SIMPLE BAROMETER

MATERIALS
- a drinking glass or tumbler
- a balloon
- an elastic band
- a drinking straw
- sticky tape
- scissors
- a strip of card 20 cm x 5 cm
- a wooden base
- a pencil

1. Cut out a piece of balloon slightly larger than the open end of the tumbler. Stretch the balloon over the tumbler and secure it with an elastic band. Tape one end of the straw to the stretched top of the balloon. Cut the other end of the straw to make a point.

2. Fold the strip of card about 5 cm from the end to make a right angle, and tape it to one end of the wooden base so that the strip stands up.

3. Stand the glass at the other end of the base so that the pointed end of the straw lines up with the card. Place the barometer in a part of the house where the temperature stays the same all the time.

4. On the card, mark the level of the straw each day for one week to record changes in air pressure. A rising straw indicates an increase in atmospheric pressure, which usually means that good weather is on the way. How accurate is your barometer?

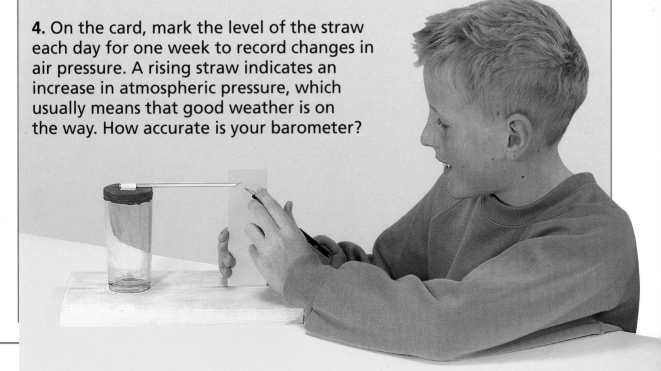

WATER PRESSURE

If you squeeze a gas, it becomes compressed. If you squeeze a bicycle pump with your finger over the end, you will find that the plunger goes in a long way because the molecules making up the air are far enough apart to be pushed closer together. If you were to fill the pump with water instead of air, you would find that the plunger hardly moves at all. Water molecules have very little space between them, so they cannot easily be compressed.

When you push on a liquid in a pipe, it is like pushing on a solid rod. Because liquids cannot be compressed, the force acting on them at one end of the pipe is passed on all the way to the other end. When a system of pipes containing a liquid is used to carry a force from one place to another, it is called a hydraulic system. 'Hydraulic' means 'to do with water'.

Hydraulic systems are very common. They are used to make car brakes work, for example, and to lift the buckets on mechanical diggers. The hydraulic systems in these machines do

not use water – they use a special oil, contained in pipes which link two or more cylinders. Each cylinder has a piston that fits tightly into the end and moves up and down when the oil pushes or pulls against it.

The law of hydraulics says that if you exert a particular pressure over a large area, you produce a greater force than if you exert the same pressure over a small area. So, to stop a car, the driver pushes on the brake pedal which presses against a small piston inside a 'master' cylinder of brake fluid. The fluid passes on the force through pipes to the brakes, where larger pistons, inside 'slave' cylinders, produce a larger force on the brake shoes or pads. These push against the wheels and slow the car down.

Hydraulic power is used to lift heavy loads.

WEIGHT LIFTER

1. Blow up the balloon and let it down several times so that it is stretched. Pull the end of the balloon over one end of the plastic pipe and seal the join with sticky tape.

2. Cut the top off the plastic bottle and cut a hole in the side, near the base. Push the balloon on the end of the pipe through the hole.

3. Tape the funnel to the other end of the tube.

4. Place the can on top of the balloon in the bottle, and put the book or brick on top of the can.

MATERIALS

- a plastic bottle
- a balloon
- a plastic tube
- a funnel
- an empty can that is narrower than the bottle
- sticky tape
- scissors
- a jug of water
- a heavy book, or brick

WARNING!

- Take care when cutting the plastic bottle.

Did you know?

The five arms of a starfish are covered with flexible, hollow 'tube feet' filled with water. The starfish can pump water in and out of these feet so that they straighten or bend. In this way, the starfish creeps across the seabed using hydraulic power.

5. Keeping the funnel higher than the book or the brick, start pouring water into the funnel. Watch the balloon begin to swell and lift the can and the weight on top. How high can you lift the weight using water power?

FLOATING AND SINKING

When you get into the bath, you may notice that the water level rises. By getting into the bath, you push some of the water out of the way. This is called *displacement*. If you could measure the volume of the water you have displaced, you would find that it is the same as the volume of your body. If you dangle a stone in water, it weighs less than if you weigh it out of water. Where has the 'missing' weight gone?

There is a force that supports objects in water and in other fluids, such as a balloon in air. The force is *upthrust*. The deeper you go, whether into the ocean depths or to the 'bottom' of the atmosphere (sea level), the greater the pressure. Upthrust is produced because the pressure of a fluid is greater at the bottom of an object than it is at the top, so the object is pushed upwards. The size of the upthrust force is the same as the weight of the fluid that the object displaces.

For an object to float in water or in air, it must generate at least as much upthrust as its own weight. For example, a ship must displace a volume of water that weighs more than itself. Ships are usually made of steel, so they must have hollow shapes to displace as much water as possible. If a ship is overloaded, its weight will be greater

Balloons float because the upthrust force on them from the air is greater than their own weight.

than the upthrust force, and it will sink. This is why there are markings, called Plimsoll lines, on the sides of ships; these show the lowest level at which it is safe for a ship to float.

Did you know?

When a submarine needs to dive, it takes in water into special tanks. The water increases the weight of the submarine so that it is no longer supported by upthrust, and sinks. When the submarine needs to rise to the surface again, water is pumped out of the tanks.

FLOATING CARGO

1. Cut three rectangular sheets of foil, each measuring 20 cm x 15 cm. You are going to construct three boat hulls from these sheets.

2. Take the first sheet of foil and fold up each side by 1 cm. Bend each corner at right angles and stick it down with tape to make a watertight seal. You now have a shallow foil 'hull' that you can load with cargo.

3. Repeat step **2** with the other sheets of foil, but fold up each side of the second sheet by 2 cm and the third by 3 cm. You will then have three boat shapes with the same mass, but they will displace different amounts of water. This will make the floating test fair.

4. Half fill the bowl with water and place the first boat on the surface. Carefully put the first weight into the centre of the hull and carry on adding weights, one at a time, to all parts of the boat until it sinks. Write down the number of weights the boat can support.

5. Repeat the test for the other foil boats. Measure the area of the boats that is in contact with the water (by multiplying the length by the width). What is the link between the number of weights that can be supported by a boat and the area of the base of each hull?

MAKING TASKS EASIER

We use machines to make tasks easier. Machines magnify the forces we exert with our muscles so that we can move objects that would otherwise be too heavy for us. Most of the machines we use are operated by *levers* or *pulleys*. These are useful where a small force moving over a great distance is needed to move a much heavier load over a short distance.

Levers are found in tools as varied as scissors, screwdrivers, wheelbarrows,

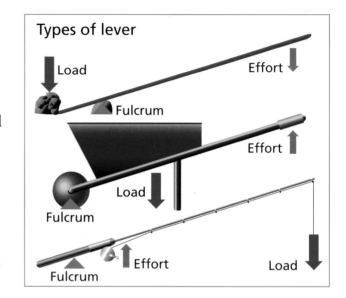

Types of lever

Load
Effort
Fulcrum

Effort
Load
Fulcrum

Effort
Load
Fulcrum

CATAPULT

1. Drill holes 3 cm apart along the lengths of square-section wood. The holes in the two uprights (the 20 cm lengths) should line up and be big enough to fit the dowel rod.

2. Stand the uprights on the baseboard and nail them into position with the panel pins. Nail the hardboard triangles to the uprights and the baseboard for support.

3. Fix the plastic cup to one end of the 30 cm length of wood, using a drawing pin. Hold this length between the uprights and push the dowel rod through one set of the holes, if necessary securing it at each end with a drawing pin. The dowel is the fulcrum of the catapult lever.

MATERIALS

- a plastic drinking cup
- 2 x 20 cm lengths and 1 x 30 cm length of 2 cm square-section wood
- a 30 cm x 12 cm wooden base
- 2 hardboard triangles, each side measuring 10 cm
- a 12 cm length of dowel rod and a hand drill with the same diameter
- 2 screw hooks
- a thick elastic band
- drawing pins
- pieces of sponge
- watercolour paint of different colours
- a sheet of card for the target
- panel pins and a hammer

bottle-openers and weighing scales. There are three parts to any lever: the point where you exert a force, or effort; the point, or fulcrum, where the lever pivots; and the point where the load is applied. The task that a lever can do depends on the position of these three points in relation to each other.

If you wanted to lift a heavy bucket of sand to the top of a building, you would use a pulley. A pulley changes a downward pull on one end of a rope into an upward pull at the other end. With two pulleys instead of one, you can lift even more weight with the same effort. But you don't get something for nothing – the bucket will only travel half the distance that the pulleys travel!

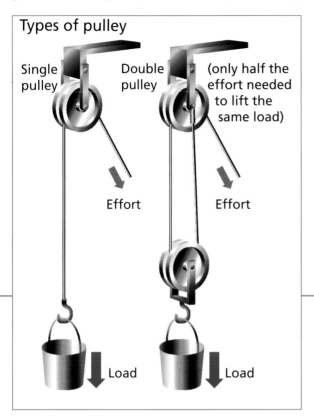

Types of pulley

Single pulley

Double pulley

(only half the effort needed to lift the same load)

Effort

Effort

Load

Load

4. Screw one hook into the other end of the 30 cm length of wood and screw the other hook into the baseboard. Fix the elastic band between the hooks.

5. Make a target with coloured zones for different scores and fit it to a wall or fence, or lay it on the ground. Soak the sponges in the paint and place one in the plastic cup. This is the load part of the catapult lever.

6. Push down on the cup end of the catapult and see the elastic band stretch. This provides the effort part of the catapult lever. Let go, and see where the paint sponge lands. Adjust your aim in order to land your sponges on the target.

7. How does changing the distance between the fulcrum and the effort affect how far the sponge load travels? Alter the position of the dowel rod to find out.

BALANCING ACT

One of the simplest levers is a playground see-saw. With this, each child takes it in turns to provide the effort to lift the other child, who is the load. You may have noticed yourself how hard it is to lift a person on the other end of a see-saw if they are heavier than you. The forces at each end are unbalanced. The only way to balance them is for the lighter child to sit further away from the fulcrum than the heavier one. With the children in these positions, a scientist would say that the turning force of the lighter child is equal to the turning force of the heavier one.

When two forces are balanced, as they are when the see-saw is horizontal, the single point around which the opposing forces turn is called the centre of gravity. Every object has a centre of gravity; it is the point where the pulling force of gravity seems to be concentrated. For example, when a gymnast is performing an exercise she knows that she must keep her centre of gravity exactly over the narrow beam. If she doesn't, the turning forces on either side of the beam will become unbalanced and she will fall off!

The centre of gravity of an object is determined by its shape and the position of most of its mass. A tall, thin object with most of its mass towards the top has a high centre of gravity. It would take only a small amount of

force to push it over. An object such as this is described as unstable. On the other hand, a short object with a wide base has a low centre of gravity. It is much harder to push over. Scientifically, you would say it is more stable.

In order to balance, this gymnast must keep her centre of gravity over the beam.

HIGH-WIRE ACT

1. Using the card, draw, colour-in and cut out a clown figure with its arms outstretched, as shown in the photograph below.

2. Cut a small notch in the head of the clown and use modelling clay to fix a washer to each hand.

3. Tie the string between the necks of the bottles and place the clown so that the string fits into the notch. The clown will balance because its centre of gravity is between its hands, below the level of the string. Give one of the bottles a sharp tap and see the clown wobble to keep his balance!

4. Try cutting out other shapes that will balance, such as this parrot.

MATERIALS
● a sheet of stiff card
● 2 metal washers
● coloured pencils
● scissors
● 50 cm of thin string
● modelling clay
● 2 bottles of water

STRONG SHAPES

Some objects are stronger than you would expect. They owe their strength to two factors: the material they are made from, and their shape. For example, if you were to stab a potato very quickly with a drinking straw, the straw would go right through it! Although a straw is easy to bend, it is very hard to squash lengthways. Cylinders, such as straws, are strong structures. A bicycle frame is made up of metal cylinders to give the bicycle strength and reduce weight. Even the bones in your own skeleton are tube-shaped.

Another shape used to strengthen structures, ranging from bicycles to bridges, is the triangle. A structure built from triangles cannot easily be twisted or collapsed. Any forces pushing down on such a building are supported by the many corners. The Eiffel Tower in Paris is made almost entirely of

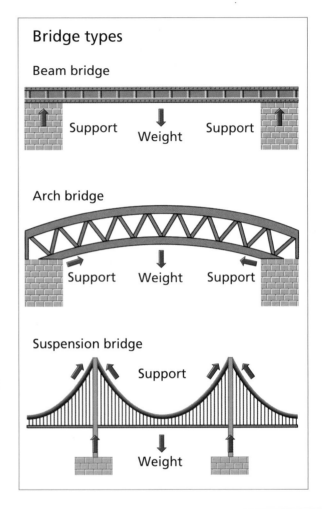

Bridge types

Beam bridge

Support   Weight   Support

Arch bridge

Support   Weight   Support

Suspension bridge

Support

Weight

BRIDGE THE GAP

1. Place the two books on a table and measure 30 cm between them. This is the distance you need to cross with your bridge.

2. Remembering what you have read about strong shapes, investigate ways of using the straws to build a bridge across the gap. Use only the smallest amounts of tape necessary to stick one bridge beam to another. The bridge mustn't obtain any strength from the sticky tape you use.

MATERIALS

- 30 x 12 cm lengths cut from paper straws (NOT bendy type)
- a ruler
- scissors
- sticky tape
- two books of equal thickness

triangles – it even has a triangular shape itself.

The science of strong shapes is perhaps best shown in the design of bridges. A properly constructed bridge must support its own weight as well as the weight of the traffic crossing it. The simplest bridges are beam bridges; these consist of a single 'span' (the distance between the bridge supports). But beam bridges cannot support their own weight beyond a certain length. Arch bridges are stronger because the arch spreads more of the weight on to the supports. Once steel and concrete became widely available, bridge builders were able to build much longer and stronger bridges, such as the modern suspension bridges. These use extremely strong steel cables to link concrete towers at each end of the bridge, or on islands. The strong shape of suspension bridges means that they can resist the downwards force of the traffic and the sideways force of high winds.

The Eiffel Tower is a strong, triangular structure with a low centre of gravity.

3. Build two bridges so that you can compare them for strength. You should think about how you are going to test the strength of the bridges when you design and build them. Include in your designs a platform of some sort for loading the bridge with weights.

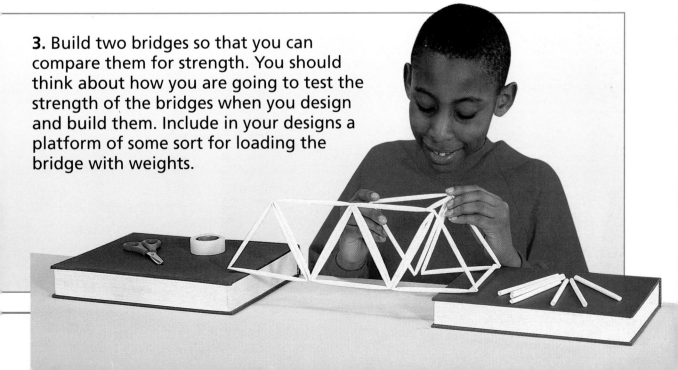

ON THE MOVE

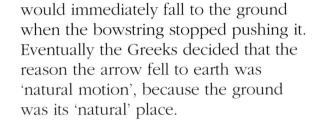

How do you make something move? If the object is not too big, you can use your muscles to exert the force required. But objects with greater mass require bigger forces, and you may need to use a machine with an engine to start them moving. Other than your own muscle force, the force that produces the most movement is gravity, which pulls objects towards the Earth.

What happens to a moving object when you stop pushing or pulling it? The ancient Greeks believed that when an arrow was fired into the air, it was the air itself that kept the arrow moving. They thought that, unless the air exerted its own force, the arrow

The energy for movement can come from many different sources.

would immediately fall to the ground when the bowstring stopped pushing it. Eventually the Greeks decided that the reason the arrow fell to earth was 'natural motion', because the ground was its 'natural' place.

It was not until the great Italian scientist Galileo began his studies of moving objects that anyone came up with a different idea. Galileo showed that once an object was moving, no extra force was needed to keep it moving. He said that an object stops moving when another force acts on it. As we have already seen, the force that acts against movement is friction. Only in deep space, away from the gravitational pull of any planet, can a rocket keep going without slowing down. Newton took Galileo's ideas further. He said not only can a force make an object move, it can also change how fast it moves and the direction in which it is moving. Newton's first law of motion states that 'an object will only move when a force acts on it, and a moving object will carry on moving at the same speed and in the same direction unless a force changes the object's speed or direction'.

MAKING THINGS MOVE

1. It is best to do this project out-of-doors, on a hard surface. Set up the ramp on the stool and draw a line across the board where it rests on the stool. This will be the start line for the ramp tests.

2. Place a toy behind the line and let it run down the slope and across the floor. How far does it go? Repeat the test twice more and work out the average distance travelled (total distance travelled in three attempts divided by 3).

3. Using the nails, fix the cotton reels about 15 cm apart on the square board. Stretch a large elastic band (you may need two bands tied together) around the reels. Pull back the elastic band to make a catapult and place a toy vehicle in it. Let go of the elastic band. How far does the vehicle go? Again, try the test several times and find out the average distance travelled.

4. Hold the toy vehicle steady with one hand and push it as hard as you can along the floor. How far does it go? Repeat as before to work out the average distance travelled.

5. Try each way of making a vehicle move with two other toys.

6. Use the squared paper and coloured pencils to make a bar chart of your measurements. From what you have read about forces and motion, can you suggest why one car goes further than the others?

MATERIALS

- a collection of small wheeled toys
- a 1 m board to act as a ramp
- a stool
- a selection of elastic bands
- a wooden board 20 cm x 20 cm
- 2 empty cotton reels
- 2 nails
- a hammer
- a long measuring tape
- squared paper
- coloured pencils
- a ruler

SPEED

When people talk about the top speed of a car being 300 kilometres per hour, they mean that the car would cover 300 kilometres if driven at that speed for one hour. Of course, cars are seldom driven in this way. It is more usual to talk about the average speed over a journey; this evens out the different speeds along the way and takes into account other traffic or poor roads.

If a car travels 100 kilometres in two hours, its average speed is worked out by dividing the distance by the time:

average speed = $\dfrac{\text{distance travelled}}{\text{time taken}}$

= $\dfrac{100}{2}$

= 50 kilometres per hour

With its sleek coat and slim body, the streamlined cheetah is the world's fastest land animal.

This speed can also be written as 50 kph or 50 km/h.

Scientists usually measure speed in metres per second (m/s) rather than

RAMP RACERS

1. In a large, open space with an even surface, arrange some books to make a stack 10 cm tall. Lean the ramp against the books and mark a line across it where it touches the books.

2. Place your car behind the line and set your stopwatch to zero. Let the car go and immediately start the stopwatch. Time how long it takes for the car to roll down the ramp, cross the floor and come to a halt.

MATERIALS

- toy cars
- a 1 m wooden ramp
- books of assorted thicknesses
- a ruler
- a stopwatch
- a long measuring tape
- a pencil

km/h, so 50 km/h would be written as 13.9 m/s (50,000 metres divided by 60, and divided by 60 again). If you walk as fast as possible, you can probably walk at around 2 m/s and run at about 5 m/s. A champion sprinter can run a 100 metre race in 10 seconds, which is a speed of 10 m/s.

The chart below shows the top air, land and sea speeds for some animals and machines.

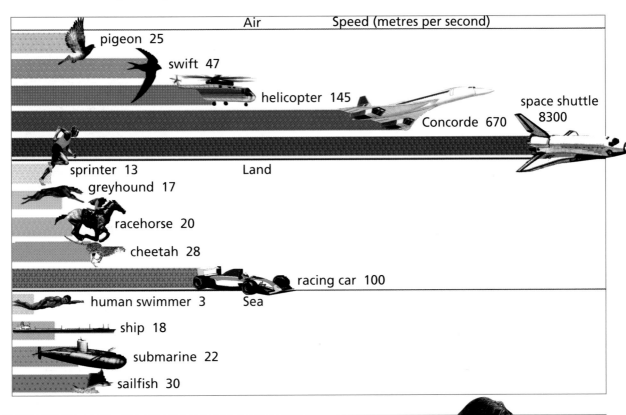

Air   Speed (metres per second)

pigeon 25

swift 47

helicopter 145

space shuttle 8300

Concorde 670

sprinter 13   Land

greyhound 17

racehorse 20

cheetah 28

racing car 100

human swimmer 3   Sea

ship 18

submarine 22

sailfish 30

3. Measure how far the car has travelled. You can now work out its average speed. Do the test again and work out the average speed for the two runs.

4. Repeat the test using more books to make ramps of different heights, say 20 cm and 30 cm. What effect does raising the height of the ramp have on the average speed of the car?

FASTER AND SLOWER

Formula 1 racing cars can accelerate from 0-150 km/h in around 3 seconds.

When you get into a car and it starts to move off, you can tell that it is going faster and faster. You feel pressed back into your seat. When the car reaches and maintains a certain speed you no longer feel pressed back. It is the same if you are travelling at 100 km/h or 200 km/h. You only experience the 'pressed back' feeling when you quickly get to – or accelerate to – a steady speed.

Acceleration describes any change in speed. You are accelerating if you speed up or if you slow down. Slowing down is sometimes called deceleration. Car manufacturers calculate the acceleration figures of their cars by knowing how long it takes to achieve a certain speed. A car that can accelerate from stationary (not moving) to 100 km/h in 10 seconds is accelerating at:

$$\frac{\text{change in speed}}{\text{time taken}} = \frac{100}{10}$$

$$= \quad 10 \text{ kilometres per hour per second, or } 10 \text{ km/h/s}$$

This means that at the end of every second of a 10-second test, the car is travelling 10 km/h faster than at the end of the second before. In the same way, when the car is slowing down, going from 100 km/h to stationary in 10 seconds, the deceleration is the same figure, although scientists might write a minus sign in front of the 10 km/h/s to show that it is a slowing-down measurement.

Did you know?
When jet fighters come in to land on an aircraft carrier, they decelerate so quickly that the pilots sometimes black out for a few seconds. The same thing can happen when a pilot ejects from an aircraft, but in this case the problem is caused by the enormous acceleration.

SPEEDY SPOTS

1. Cut off the top 5 cm of the washing-up liquid bottle and push a pin through the cap to make a small hole. Tape the cut section of the bottle to the rear of the toy. This is the reservoir.

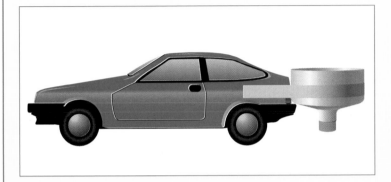

MATERIALS

- a large toy car or truck
- a 1 m wooden board
- books
- an empty washing-up liquid bottle
- glycerine
- food colouring
- a small jar
- 1 m x 10 cm strips of plain paper, such as the reverse side of plain wallpaper
- sticky tape
- modelling clay
- a pin

2. Mix a few drops of food colouring with some glycerine in a jar and pour the mixture into the reservoir. Adjust the size of the hole in the cap so that the colouring drips at about five drops per second. Seal the hole with modelling clay.

3. Tape the strip of paper on to the wooden board and place one end of the board on a stack of books. Hold the toy at the top of the slope. Remove the modelling clay and let the toy roll down the slope.

4. Reseal the hole in the cap and allow the spots on the strip to dry. What do you notice about the distance between the spots? Why do you think this is?

5. Repeat the test with the board at a steeper angle. What happens to the distance between the spots? How does the slope of the board affect the acceleration of the toy?

ACTION AND REACTION

What do rockets and runners have in common? The answer is that they both illustrate Isaac Newton's laws of motion. Take the launch of the space shuttle, for example. Before the motor fires, the shuttle is still: this illustrates the first law (that an object at rest will stay at rest until a force acts upon it). When the motor fires, the shuttle lifts off: this illustrates the second law, which says that 'when a force acts on an object, the object changes its speed or direction in the same direction as the force that has been applied'.

The space shuttle's launch demonstrates Newton's three laws of motion.

BALLOON ROCKETS

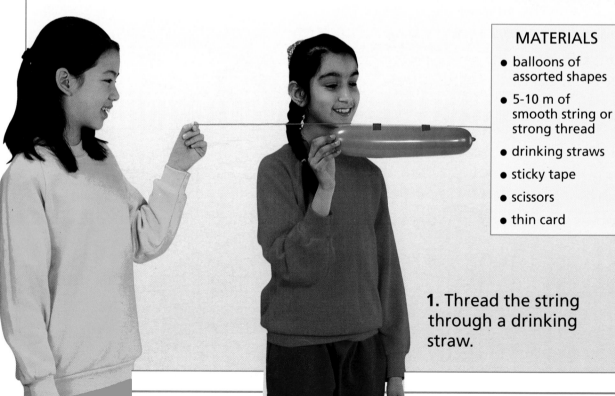

MATERIALS
- balloons of assorted shapes
- 5-10 m of smooth string or strong thread
- drinking straws
- sticky tape
- scissors
- thin card

1. Thread the string through a drinking straw.

The rocket lifts off because there is a tremendous force on it, which comes from the burning gas streaming backwards from the engines. This illustrates Newton's third law, which says that 'for every force – or action – there is an equal force – or reaction – against it'.

When you run, you may think it is your muscles that move you forward, but it is the reaction of the ground against the backwards push of your feet that is pushing with just as much force. If the ground did not produce an equal reaction force, you would sink into the ground, as if it were water.

A simple test to illustrate Newton's third law is for you and a friend to put on roller skates and stand facing each other on a smooth surface. Put your hands together and push gently, staying as upright as you can. Instead of pushing your friend away, you both roll backwards! If your friend is heavier than you, then you will roll back more than he or she does. If you are both the same weight, you will roll back the same distance.

2. Blow up the balloon and attach it with sticky tape to the straw.

3. Keeping the string taut, release the balloon. The sudden release of air is jet propulsion. How far does the balloon travel?

4. Try the test with other balloon shapes. Do some balloons make better rockets than others?

5. Try adding triangles of card as fins to stabilize the balloon in 'flight'.

COLLISIONS

When a moving ball collides with a moving bat, you would expect the ball to shoot off in a different direction and at a higher speed than before. You would also expect the bat to carry on moving in the same direction, but perhaps a bit slower. What decides that the ball will move faster after the collision, and not the bat? The two important things to consider are the speed and the mass of the ball and the bat.

Scientists combine speed and mass in one idea, called momentum. If two objects are moving towards each other at the same speed, but one has a greater mass than the other, then it has more momentum. When the objects collide, the total momentum of the two objects, added together, is shared equally between them. If their masses stay the same as before, the lighter object will go faster after the collision, while the heavier object will go slower. This is one of the laws of science, and it is called the law of conservation of momentum (conservation means 'to stay the same').

Every day, collisions occur that show what damage the law of conservation of momentum can do. These are road accidents and accidents that occur during sports and games when the players are not using protective clothing or equipment.

These American football players wear special clothing to protect themselves in collisions.

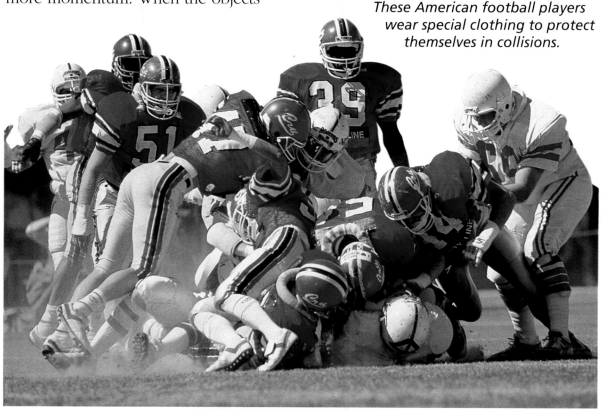

MINI POOL

MATERIALS
- a large sheet of shiny card
- 9 draughts (4 black, 4 white and 1 other)
- scissors
- a ruler
- a felt-tip pen
- coloured sticky labels
- a shoe box or empty cereal box, smaller all around than the shiny card
- sticky tape

1. With the scissors, score along each side of the sheet of card, about 2 cm in from the edge. Cut a small square of card out of each corner so that the edges can be turned up and the corners taped. This is your pool table.

2. Cut a hole in each corner of the 'table', big enough to let a draught fall through. Put the 'table' on the empty box.

3. Draw a coloured spot on one of the draughts using the pen or a coloured label and place it near the edge of the 'table'. Use pieces of sticky label to number each set of draughts from 1-4. These are the points values of each draught. Place the eight numbered draughts in the centre of the table.

4. With a friend, take a set of draughts each. Take it in turns to knock each other's draughts into a corner 'pocket' by flicking the coloured draught so that it strikes either a black or a white draught. Record the number of points, and have an extra go whenever you 'pot' a draught.

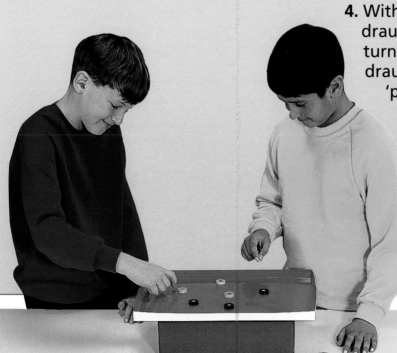

ROUND AND ROUND

If you swing a bucket of water in a circle, the water will not spill out (as long as the bucket is moving fast enough!). This is because the water is pushing against the bucket as the bucket tries to travel in a straight line. Remember, Newton's first law says that a moving object will continue in a straight line unless acted upon by a force. (If you let go of the bucket, you would provide this force!) You have to pull on the handle of the bucket to

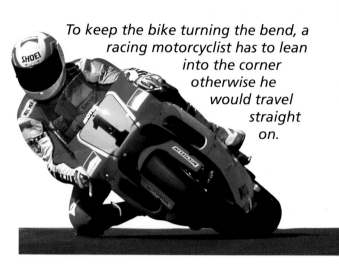

To keep the bike turning the bend, a racing motorcyclist has to lean into the corner otherwise he would travel straight on.

LOOP THE LOOP

1. Cut the sheet of card into four or five strips, 50 cm x 6 cm each. Score two lines along the length of each strip, so that the edges can be folded up to make a U-shaped track 2-3 cm wide. These are the sections that you will join up to make your roller-coaster ride!

2. Make vertical cuts every 2-3 cm along the sides of two of the track sections. Line up the cuts on one side with those on the opposite side.

3. Bend the tracks so that the cuts overlap. Tape across the cuts to shape each track into a semicircle. Depending on the stiffness of your card and the closeness of the cuts, you may be able to make almost complete circles out of both sections of track.

4. Use sticky tape to assemble the sections of track so that the end of one is raised much higher than the rest. Make sure that no sticky tape is showing on the inside of the track, as this could slow the marble down. The completed track should start with a straight section, lead into one or two loops and finish with another straight section.

MATERIALS
- a large sheet of thin card 50 cm square
- a ruler
- scissors
- sticky tape
- marbles of different sizes

WARNING
- Take care when scoring the card.

keep it moving in a circle. The force you exert on the bucket is called centripetal force. This force is constantly making the bucket change direction, turning in towards the centre of the circle – you! The faster you swing the bucket, the greater is the centripetal force you need to exert to keep it moving.

People often confuse centripetal force with a force that seems to push things out from the centre: this is called centrifugal force. In fact, centrifugal force does not exist – it is just the natural resistance, or inertia, of an object to changing its speed or direction.

Did you know?

When you see pictures of astronauts 'walking' in space, they are actually falling towards the Earth! The reason is that Earth's gravity is continually pulling them, but their momentum from being shot into space is forwards, in a straight line away from the Earth. The result is that the astronauts 'fall' in a circular orbit around the planet.

5. Hold a marble at the top of the first section and let it go. Does it loop the loop? You may need to adjust the size of the loop or the height of the first section so that the marble gets to the end of the track. Which marbles loop the loop best: the heavier or the lighter ones? How can you make the marbles travel faster down the track?

GLOSSARY

Acceleration A change in speed or direction.

Atmospheric pressure Pressure exerted by the movement of gas molecules in the atmosphere.

Barometer A device for measuring air pressure.

Centre of gravity The point at which the mass of an object seems to be concentrated.

Centripetal force The force that keeps a rotating object moving in a circle.

Conservation of momentum The principle that momentum is never lost. Momentum is calculated by multiplying the mass of an object by its speed. When two objects collide the sum of their momentum after the collision is the same as the sum of their momentum before the collision.

Drag The tendency for air or a liquid to slow a moving object.

Force A push, pull or turn. Something that changes the shape or motion of an object.

Friction The force that resists movement when one surface slides over another.

Fulcrum The point at which a lever pivots.

Gravity The force of attraction between two objects. The size of the force depends on the mass of the object.

Hydraulics The transfer of force through a liquid.

Inertia An object's resistance to movement or a change in motion.

Lever A simple machine that reduces the effort needed to lift a load. A lever consists of a rigid beam turning around a fulcrum.

Mass The measure of an amount of matter. Wherever the measurement is made, an object's mass does not change.

Momentum see **Conservation of momentum**.

Pressure The force exerted over a particular area.

Speed The rate at which an object moves. Average speed is found by dividing the distance travelled by the time taken.

Surface tension A force that tends to pull the surface of a liquid into the smallest possible area, usually a sphere, like a raindrop.

Thrust The force that propels a rocket or an aircraft.

Weight A measure of the force of gravity acting on a mass.

FURTHER INFORMATION

BOOKS

Eyewitness Science: Force and Motion Peter Lafferty (Dorling Kindersley, 1992)

How Science Works Judith Hann (Dorling Kindersley, 1991)

How Things Work Neil Ardley (Dorling Kindersley, 1995)

How Things Work Chris Oxlade (Zigzag, 1995)

Kingfisher Book of How Things Work Steve Parker (Kingfisher, 1990)

The Macmillan Book of How Things Work Michael and Marcia Folsom (Aladdin Books, 1987)

Make it Work! Machines David Glover (Two-Can, 1993)

My Science Book Of...Gravity, Machines, Movement Neil Ardley (Dorling Kindersley, 1992)

The Oxford Children's Book of Science (Oxford University Press, 1994)

Usborne Introduction to Physics Amanda Kent and Alan Ward (Usborne, 1983)

CD–ROMS

The Way Things Work David Macaulay (Dorling Kindersley, 1988)

ANSWERS TO QUESTIONS

Answers to questions posed in the projects.

Pages 6-7 Both balls hit the clay at the same time. Weight does not affect the speed of the balls. The heavier ball will have made a deeper/wider dent. The size of an object does not affect the speed at which it falls, provided that the object's weight is much greater than the force of air resistance.

Pages 10-11 Silver Dancers: The ball will jump away to another groove on the disc. Water Magic: The water stream will bend towards the ruler which attracts the positive charge on the water molecules.

Pages 12-13 Generally springs are more accurate than elastic bands; they will be more reliable over several measurements.

Pages 14-15 Shiny, smooth materials, such as plastic or leather, have a low friction force. Rough, 'sticky' materials, such as rubber and carpet, have a high friction force. On the soles of the shoes, a zig-zag pattern of cuts gives more friction force.

Pages 16-17 A square or rectangular hull has most drag, while a pointed, triangular shape is most streamlined,

Pages 18-19 Bending the flaps will make the plane swoop up or down. Bending the rudder will turn it left or right.

Pages 26-27 The greater the area of the base of the boat, the more weights that can be supported.

Pages 28-29 The greater the distance between the fulcrum and the effort, the further the sponge load travels.

Pages 34-35 One car will go further than another if there is less friction between the wheels and the surface (the board or the floor), or if it has a more streamlined shape, or is lighter.

Pages 36-37 The steeper the ramp, the greater the average speed of the cars.

Pages 38-39 The distance between the ink spots increases because the car is moving further in the time between each drop. With the board at a steeper angle, the distance between the spots increases even more because the car accelerates faster as the slope is made steeper.

Pages 44-45 Within broad limits, the lighter (smaller) marbles will loop the loop better than heavier (larger) marbles. Raise the end of the track to increase the speed of the marbles, or flick them with a finger.

INDEX